ISBN 13: 978-1-931945-78-3
ISBN 10: 1-931945-78-0

Library of Congress Catalog Number: 2007930480

Printed in South Korea

First Printing: July 2007

11 10 09 08 07   5 4 3 2 1

Andover, Minnesota

Expert Publishing, Inc.
14314 Thrush Street NW,
Andover, MN 55304-3330
1-877-755-4966
www.expertpublishinginc.com

Diane Hagler Photography
1001 Lavon Lane
Burnsville, Minnesota 55306
952-432-2236
www.dianehaglerphotography.com
www.rustyscards.com

Dedication

To Rusty, my Cavalier King Charles Spaniel and creative outlet.

Acknowledgements

My thanks to Rusty, my faithful companion, who is always ready for a photo shoot.

My husband, Gary, for his love, support, and putting up with my crazy ideas.

My parents for making their old Brownie Box camera
available to me at an early age.

The Wednesday Night Girls for their humor, support, and encouragement.

My photo assistants for putting up with dog hair in the studio.

Thanks to Bill Von Bank for always promoting my work.

Many thanks also to Rusty's Fan Club, my fellow photographers, friends, family,
and clients who have always enjoyed Rusty's photos.

SiT HAPPENS

Roses are Red, Violets are Blue

If I wasn't neutered, I'd be after you.

Rub a Dub Doggy

I've Got
a Bone To Pick
With You!

Mini Me

Billy
Bob
Rusty

Eat, Drink, & be Hairy

Moving Day Bites

THE
COOK
IS NOT

RESPONSIBLE
FOR
HAIR
IN
FOOD

Beauty Is More Than "Fur" Deep

Congratulations

Ears
to
You!

All I Need Now is a Pet-i-cure

Sometimes ... Just
"Letting Go"
Is
A Good Thing

RUN,
ROMP,
&
RACE
DAILY

Lick or Treat

Let's
Party

If Friends
Were
Flowers...

I'd Pick
You

Who Let The Dogs Out ?

Happiness is What's on the Other Side of the Door

Congratulations

On Your New
Addition to the Pack

In Your Easter Bonnet...

Cele-bark With Friends

Bite Me, Pilgrim

Hot Under The Collar?

Take A Dip!

Then Comes Rusty
In The Baby Carriage

How to Get Stuffed
at the Table

An Apple
a Day
Keeps the Vet
Away

APPLES

10¢ ea.

Ho
Ho...

Woofin' Ho

A Kiss From a Dog
Will Never Give
You a Cold

Where's ~~Waldo~~ Rusty ?

Every
Dog

Has His
Day

Thanks
For
Being
An
Angel

Four Legged Table Manners

A Cute Little Tail
Attracts a Lot of Attention

SOME PEOPLE WOULD NEVER GO FOR WALKS.

Spring Has Sprung,
the Grass is Green,

I'm the Cutest Hound You've Ever Seen.

Live
Well

Laugh
Often

Lick
Much

Diane Hagler
(M. Photog., Cr., A–MPAA)

Diane Hagler, originally from Cincinnati, Ohio, resides in Burnsville, Minnesota, with her husband, Gary, and her two Cavalier King Charles Spaniels, Rusty and Cooper. She owns and operates a photography studio specializing in children, families, high school seniors, and, of course, pets. Photography has been a passion of Diane's since the seventh grade and she continues to advance in the new digital age. She has won many regional, national, and state awards, including the prestigious "Dworshak" award for the highest scoring print in Minnesota. She is a Master Craftsmen in Photography with the Professional Photographers of America and Accredited in the State of Minnesota.

Rusty & Diane

MY DOG ISN'T SPOILED...
I'M JUST WELL TRAINED.

Contact

Diane Hagler

1001 Lavon Lane ✖ Burnsville, Minnesota 55306 ✖ 952 432-2236
www.dianehaglerphotography.com ✖ www.rustyscards.com